Unbreakable Spirits

Christine Groethe

Unbreakable Spirits: Narratives and Stories of Resilience from Women Who Have Escaped Early Marriages in Mexico

All rights reserved

Copyright © 2023 by **Christine Groethe**

No part of this publication may be reproduced, distributed, or transmitted in any form or by any means, including photocopying, recording, or other electronic or mechanical methods, without the prior written permission of the publisher, except in the case of brief quotations embodied in critical reviews and certain other noncommercial uses permitted by copyright law.

Published by BooxAi

ISBN: 978-965-578-699-6

Unbreakable Spirits

Narratives and Stories of Resilience from Women Who Have Escaped Early Marriages in Mexico

Christine Groethe

Contents

CHAPTER 1   7
The Cultural Significance of Age Disparities in Mexican Marriages

CHAPTER 2   15
The Role of Family and Community in Early Mexican Weddings

CHAPTER 3   23
Emotional and Psychological Impacts on Young Girls Forced into Early Marriages in Mexico

CHAPTER 4   31
Advocacy and Support Organizations for Girls Affected by Early Marriages in Mexico

CHAPTER 5   41
Narratives and Stories of Resilience from Women Who Have Escaped Early Marriages in Mexico

CONCLUSION   49
A Call to Action for Ending Early Marriages in Mexico

TESTIMONIAL I   53
Maria's story

Betrothal   53
The Weight of Expectations   54
The Arrival of Womanhood   55

TESTIMONIAL II   57
Jessica's Story

The Decision   57
A Heartfelt Conversation   58
Setting Out   59

Chapter One
The Cultural Significance of Age Disparities in Mexican Marriages

Historical Context of Early Marriages in Mexico
In order to understand the cultural significance of age disparities in Mexican marriages, it is important to delve into the historical context of early marriages in Mexico. For centuries, it has been a common practice for young girls to be married off at a very young age, often before they even reach puberty. This tradition has been deeply rooted in the country's social and cultural fabric.

The role of family and community in early Mexican weddings cannot be overstated. Marriage is considered a communal affair, and decisions regarding a young girl's marriage are made collectively by her family and the wider community. These decisions are influenced by factors such as economic considerations, social status, and cultural norms. The family's reputation and honor are often tied to the girl's compliance with the arranged marriage.

However, the emotional and psychological impacts on young girls forced into early marriages in Mexico are immense. These girls are robbed of their childhood and forced to take on adult responsibilities at an age when they should be focused on education and personal growth. They often suffer from low self-esteem, depression, and a sense of powerlessness. Many of them are subjected to domestic violence and sexual abuse within their marriages, leading to further trauma and emotional scars.

Fortunately, there are advocacy and support organizations for girls affected by early marriages in Mexico. These organizations work tirelessly to provide legal aid, counseling, and educational opportunities for these girls. They also raise awareness about the negative consequences of early marriages and advocate for policy changes to protect the rights of young girls.

"Unbreakable Spirits: Narratives and Stories of Resilience from Women Who Have Escaped Early Marriages in Mexico" is a collection of powerful narratives and stories from women who have managed to escape early marriages. These women share their experiences of survival, resilience, and triumph over adversity. Their stories serve as a source of inspiration and hope for others who may find themselves trapped in similar situations.

By shedding light on the historical context, cultural significance, and personal experiences related to early marriages in Mexico, this subchapter aims to raise awareness among a wide audience. It is crucial for everyone to understand the complexities surrounding this issue and the urgent need for change. Only through collective action and support can we break the cycle of early marriages and empower young girls to fulfill their potential.

Traditional Beliefs and Cultural Norms Surrounding Age Disparities

In the subchapter "Traditional Beliefs and Cultural Norms Surrounding Age Disparities," we delve into the deep-rooted cultural significance of age disparities in Mexican marriages. This chapter explores the role of family and community in early Mexican weddings, the emotional and psychological impacts on young girls forced into early marriages, and sheds light on advocacy and support organizations for girls affected by this practice. Furthermore, we share narratives and stories of resilience from women who have escaped early marriages in Mexico, shedding light on their journeys to freedom.

Age disparities in Mexican marriages have long been entrenched in traditional beliefs and cultural norms. In many rural areas of Mexico, it is customary for girls as young as 12 or 13 to be married off to older men. This practice is often justified by the belief that marrying young ensures a woman's purity and increases her chances of bearing children. However, the consequences of these age disparities are far-reaching and detrimental.

Family and community play a significant role in perpetuating early marriages in Mexico. Parents may view marrying off their daughters at a young age as a way to secure their economic future or maintain family honor. The community, on the other hand, may exert pressure to conform to these norms, further reinforcing the cycle.

The emotional and psychological impacts on young girls forced into early marriages are profound. These girls are abruptly stripped of their childhood and forced into adult responsibilities, often without proper education or life skills. They face social isolation, limited opportunities for personal growth, and an increased risk of domestic violence and abuse. The weight of these burdens can have long-lasting effects on their mental health and well-being.

Fortunately, there are advocacy and support organizations in Mexico working tirelessly to address this pressing issue. These organizations provide counseling, legal assistance, and educational opportunities to girls affected by early marriages. They also advocate for policy changes and raise awareness within communities to challenge and change these harmful cultural norms.

The subchapter also includes narratives and stories of

resilience from women who have managed to escape early marriages. These women share their personal journeys, their struggles, and triumphs. Their stories serve as a testament to the indomitable spirit of these women and inspire others to break free from the shackles of early marriages.

"Traditional Beliefs and Cultural Norms Surrounding Age Disparities" sheds light on the cultural significance of age disparities, the role of family and community, the emotional and psychological impacts, advocacy and support organizations, and narratives of resilience. This chapter aims to raise awareness and foster dialogue surrounding this issue in the hopes of bringing about lasting change and empowerment for girls affected by early marriages in Mexico.

Societal Perceptions and Attitudes Towards Early Marriages

In Mexico, the cultural significance of age disparities in marriages has long been a topic of discussion. Traditionally, it has been widely accepted for young girls to be married off at an early age, often to much older men. This practice is deeply ingrained in Mexican culture, where the role of family and community plays a significant role in the decision-making process.

The role of family and community in early Mexican weddings cannot be overstated. Parents, grandparents, and other relatives often play a central role in arranging these unions, believing that it is in the best interest of their daughters to be married off young. They view early marriage as a way to ensure their daughters' safety, protect their reputation, and secure their future. However, these perceptions fail to consider the emotional and psychological impacts on the young girls who are forced into these marriages.

The emotional and psychological impacts on young girls forced into early marriages in Mexico are devastating. These

Unbreakable Spirits

girls are robbed of their childhood, denied education, and often subjected to abuse and violence within their marriages. They face immense pressure to conform to societal expectations and fulfill their roles as wives and mothers, despite being ill-prepared for the responsibilities that come with marriage.

Thankfully, there are advocacy and support organizations in Mexico that are working tirelessly to address the issue of early marriages. These organizations provide a safe space for girls affected by early marriages, offering counseling, education, and legal support. They empower these young girls to reclaim their lives and make their own choices, breaking free from the cycle of early marriages.

"Unbreakable Spirits: Narratives and Stories of Resilience from Women Who Have Escaped Early Marriages in Mexico" aims to shed light on the experiences of these women who have escaped early marriages. Their narratives and stories of resilience serve as a testament to the strength of the human spirit and the power of hope. Through their stories, we gain a deeper understanding of the societal perceptions and attitudes towards early marriages in Mexico, and the importance of challenging and changing these perceptions.

This subchapter aims to engage a broad audience, including individuals interested in the cultural significance of age disparities in Mexican marriages, the role of family and community in early Mexican weddings, the emotional and psychological impacts on young girls forced into early marriages in Mexico, advocacy and support organizations for girls affected by early marriages in Mexico, and narratives and stories of resilience from women who have escaped early marriages in Mexico. By exploring these topics, we can collectively work towards ending the harmful practice of early marriages and creating a better future for all.

. . .

Christine Groethe

Impact of Age Disparities on Gender Dynamics and Power Imbalance

In the culturally rich country of Mexico, age disparities in marriages play a significant role in shaping gender dynamics and creating power imbalances within relationships. This subchapter delves into the various aspects of this issue and its consequences on women who have escaped early marriages. Understanding the cultural significance of age disparities in Mexican marriages is essential to comprehend the complexities surrounding this practice.

Mexican society places great importance on age as a marker of authority and respect. In traditional Mexican families, older individuals are revered and often hold significant decision-making power. This cultural norm is reflected in marriages, where age differences contribute to the unequal distribution of power between spouses. Young girls forced into early marriages often find themselves in relationships where they lack agency and are subjected to the dominance of their older partners.

The role of family and community in early Mexican weddings cannot be overlooked. Families play a crucial role in arranging marriages, and community members often reinforce these practices. The pressure to conform to societal expectations can be overwhelming for young girls, who may face limited options if they resist early marriages. This social control perpetuates the power imbalance within relationships and creates a cycle that is difficult to break.

The emotional and psychological impacts on young girls forced into early marriages in Mexico are profound. These girls are often deprived of their childhood, education, and personal development. They face increased risks of physical and sexual abuse, as well as limited social and economic opportunities. The long-term psychological effects can include low self-esteem, depression, and anxiety. It is crucial to shed light on these consequences to advocate for change and support girls affected by early marriages.

Fortunately, advocacy and support organizations have emerged to address this pressing issue in Mexico. These organizations work tirelessly to raise awareness, provide resources, and empower young girls to escape early marriages. Their efforts contribute to dismantling the power imbalances and promoting gender equality within relationships.

The heart of this subchapter lies in the narratives and stories of resilience from women who have escaped early marriages in Mexico. These brave women share their experiences, challenges, and triumphs, offering inspiration and hope to others facing similar situations. By amplifying their voices, we aim to break the cycle of early marriages and empower young girls to reclaim their lives.

In conclusion, the impact of age disparities on gender dynamics and power imbalance in Mexican marriages is a critical issue that affects countless young girls. By exploring the cultural significance, the role of family and community, the emotional and psychological impacts, advocacy and support organizations, and the narratives of resilience, we can shed light on this complex topic and work towards a more equitable and empowering future for all.

Chapter Two
The Role of Family and Community in Early Mexican Weddings

Family Influence and Decision-making in Arranged Marriages
In the context of early marriages in Mexico, the role of family influence and decision-making is a significant factor that shapes the lives of young girls. Arranged marriages, often orchestrated by parents or other family members, can have profound consequences for these girls, shaping their futures and impacting their emotional and psychological well-being.

The cultural significance of age disparities in Mexican marriages plays a crucial role in understanding the dynamics of arranged marriages. In many traditional Mexican communities, it is not uncommon for older men to marry younger girls, sometimes as young as 12 or 13 years old. This age disparity is seen as a reflection of power imbalances and gender inequality within the society. Exploring this cultural significance helps shed light on the social norms and expectations that perpetuate early marriages.

Within the context of arranged marriages, the role of family and community is paramount. The decisions regarding whom a young girl will marry are often made by her parents or other

Christine Groethe

family members, who consider factors such as social status, economic stability, and cultural compatibility. The influence of family and community in these decisions can limit a girl's agency and autonomy, often disregarding her own wishes and dreams.

The emotional and psychological impacts on young girls forced into early marriages in Mexico can be devastating. These girls are often subjected to a loss of childhood, education, and personal development. They may experience feelings of isolation, depression, and anxiety as they are thrust into adult roles and responsibilities at a tender age. Exploring these impacts helps raise awareness about the need for support and intervention for girls affected by early marriages.

Fortunately, there are advocacy and support organizations in Mexico working tirelessly to address the issue of early marriages. These organizations provide resources, counseling, and legal assistance to girls who have been forced into these marriages, empowering them to escape and rebuild their lives. Sharing stories of resilience from women who have escaped early marriages in Mexico can inspire others and highlight the strength and determination of these women.

In conclusion, the influence of family and decision-making in arranged marriages is a critical aspect of understanding early marriages in Mexico. By delving into the cultural significance of age disparities, the role of family and community, and the emotional and psychological impacts on young girls, we can raise awareness, advocate for change, and support organizations working towards ending early marriages in Mexico. The narratives and stories of resilience from women who have escaped these marriages serve as a testament to the human spirit and the power of resilience.

Community Expectations and Pressure on Young Girls to Marry

Unbreakable Spirits

In the patriarchal society of Mexico, the cultural significance of age disparities in marriages is deeply rooted. From a young age, girls are conditioned to believe that their ultimate purpose in life is to get married and start a family. As they enter adolescence, the pressure from their families and communities to find a suitable husband becomes overwhelming.

The role of family and community in early Mexican weddings cannot be underestimated. Families view marriage as a way to preserve their honor and reputation, often disregarding the wishes and aspirations of their daughters. The community, on the other hand, enforces these expectations and perpetuates the notion that a girl's worth lies solely in her ability to secure a husband.

The emotional and psychological impacts on young girls forced into early marriages in Mexico are devastating. These girls are robbed of their childhood and denied the opportunity to pursue education and personal growth. Many suffer from low self-esteem, depression, and anxiety as they struggle to navigate the challenges of married life at such a tender age.

Fortunately, there are advocacy and support organizations that have emerged to address the issue of early marriages in Mexico. These organizations provide girls with the necessary resources and tools to escape abusive or unwanted marriages. They offer counseling, legal aid, and educational opportunities to help these girls reclaim their lives and build a brighter future.

"Unbreakable Spirits: Narratives and Stories of Resilience from Women Who Have Escaped Early Marriages in Mexico" is a powerful collection of stories that sheds light on the strength and resilience of these women. Through their narratives, readers gain insight into the harsh realities they faced and the obstacles they overcame to break free from the chains of early marriage.

These stories serve as a testament to the indomitable spirit of these women and inspire others to take action against the oppressive societal norms that perpetuate early marriages. By sharing their experiences, these women not only raise awareness but also provide a sense of hope and empowerment to those who may be trapped in similar situations.

"Unbreakable Spirits" is a must-read for everyone who seeks to understand the cultural complexities surrounding early marriages in Mexico. It is a call to action, urging society to challenge and dismantle the expectations and pressures that force young girls into marriages before they are ready. Through education, advocacy, and support, we can create a future where every girl has the freedom to choose her own path and fulfill her dreams.

Rituals and Traditions Associated with Early Mexican Weddings

Mexican weddings are steeped in rich traditions and rituals that have been passed down through generations. These rituals and traditions hold deep cultural significance and are a reflection of the values and beliefs of the Mexican people. Early Mexican weddings, particularly those involving young girls, are no exception to this.

One of the most prominent rituals associated with early Mexican weddings is the Quinceañera. This celebration marks a girl's transition from childhood to womanhood. It is typically held on her fifteenth birthday and is a grand event that involves family, friends, and the entire community. The Quinceañera is a symbol of a young girl's readiness for marriage and is often seen as a precursor to an early wedding.

Another important tradition is the exchange of vows and rings. Just like in any other wedding, the couple exchanges vows to signify their commitment to each other. However, in early Mexican weddings, the rings hold a special significance. They are often passed down through generations, symbolizing the continuity and strength of the family unit.

Unbreakable Spirits

Family and community play a crucial role in early Mexican weddings. The support and involvement of loved ones are seen as essential for the success of the marriage. The families of both the bride and groom come together to plan and organize the wedding, ensuring that all customs and traditions are followed. The community also plays a part by offering guidance and support to the young couple as they embark on their journey together.

However, behind the colorful and joyous facade of early Mexican weddings, there are emotional and psychological impacts on young girls forced into these marriages. Many girls are forced to leave school and abandon their dreams, facing a life of limited opportunities and potential. The pressure to conform to societal norms and expectations can lead to feelings of isolation, depression, and even abuse.

Thankfully, there are advocacy and support organizations dedicated to helping girls affected by early marriages in Mexico. These organizations provide a safe space for girls to share their stories, receive counseling, and access educational opportunities. They empower these young women to break free from the chains of early marriages and build a brighter future for themselves.

"Unbreakable Spirits: Narratives and Stories of Resilience from Women Who Have Escaped Early Marriages in Mexico" is a collection of stories that highlight the strength and resilience of these women. Through their narratives, they inspire others to overcome adversity and seek a life of freedom and fulfillment.

In conclusion, early Mexican weddings are deeply rooted in rituals and traditions that reflect the cultural significance of age disparities in marriages. While these ceremonies may seem festive on the surface, there are emotional and psychological impacts on young girls forced into these unions. However, the tireless work of advocacy and support organizations, coupled with the narratives of resilient women, offers hope for a brighter future for those affected by early marriages in Mexico.

Christine Groethe

. . .

Interplay Between Family Support and Societal Constraints

In the context of early marriages in Mexico, the interplay between family support and societal constraints is a crucial aspect that shapes the experiences of young girls. This subchapter explores how the cultural significance of age disparities in Mexican marriages, the role of family and community, and the emotional and psychological impacts intertwine to create a complex web of challenges and resilience.

In Mexican society, age disparities in marriages have deep cultural roots. It is not uncommon for young girls to be married off to older men, often due to economic and social pressures. The cultural significance of these age disparities perpetuates societal norms and expectations, making it difficult for young girls to escape the cycle of early marriages. This subchapter delves into the historical and cultural factors that contribute to the acceptance of such unions, shedding light on the underlying dynamics of this issue.

Family and community play a significant role in early Mexican weddings. While some families may actively support and encourage early marriages, others may be trapped in a cycle of poverty and lack of education, perpetuating the practice. This subchapter examines how family dynamics, economic factors, and social pressures influence the decision-making process surrounding early marriages. It also explores the potential for change and the role of supportive families in empowering young girls to break free from this harmful tradition.

The emotional and psychological impacts on young girls forced into early marriages are immense. This subchapter uncovers the detrimental effects of these unions, such as limited educational opportunities, increased vulnerability to domestic violence, and the loss of childhood. It also highlights the resilience and strength of these young women, who manage to

Unbreakable Spirits

overcome adversity and find their voices in the face of societal constraints.

Advocacy and support organizations play a vital role in addressing the challenges faced by girls affected by early marriages in Mexico. This subchapter explores the work of these organizations, providing information on the resources and services they offer. It also highlights the importance of community engagement and awareness in bringing about long-term change.

Lastly, this subchapter presents narratives and stories of resilience from women who have escaped early marriages in Mexico. These first-hand accounts offer powerful insights into the struggles, triumphs, and lessons learned from their experiences. By sharing these stories, this chapter aims to inspire and empower others to break free from the confines of early marriages and create a better future for themselves and future generations.

Overall, this subchapter delves into the complex interplay between family support and societal constraints in the context of early marriages in Mexico. It aims to shed light on the cultural significance of age disparities, the role of family and community, the emotional and psychological impacts, advocacy and support organizations, and the narratives of resilience. By understanding these dynamics, we can work towards a society where every girl has the opportunity to thrive and fulfill her potential.

Chapter Three
Emotional and Psychological Impacts on Young Girls Forced into Early Marriages in Mexico

Loss of Childhood and Educational Opportunities

In the book "Unbreakable Spirits: Narratives and Stories of Resilience from Women Who Have Escaped Early Marriages in Mexico," we delve into the heart-wrenching topic of early marriages in Mexico. This subchapter explores the harrowing consequences of these unions on the affected girls' childhood and educational opportunities.

The cultural significance of age disparities in Mexican marriages cannot be underestimated. Traditional gender roles, societal expectations, and economic factors often lead to young girls being forced into marriages with older men. This cultural phenomenon perpetuates a cycle of inequality and denies these girls the chance to experience a normal childhood.

When a young girl is married off, her dreams and aspirations are abruptly halted. She is thrust into a role of a wife and a mother, prematurely burdened with adult responsibilities. The loss of her childhood is irreparable, as she is deprived of the opportunity to play, learn, and grow at her own pace. Instead, she becomes entangled in a marital life that she is not ready for, sacrificing her education in the process.

Christine Groethe

Education is a fundamental right that every child should have access to. However, early marriages in Mexico often result in girls dropping out of school. This denies them the chance to acquire knowledge, develop critical thinking skills, and gain economic independence. Without an education, these girls are more likely to remain trapped in cycles of poverty, unable to break free from the limitations imposed upon them.

The emotional and psychological impacts on young girls forced into early marriages in Mexico are profound. They endure immense pressure, isolation, and abuse within their marital homes. The lack of emotional maturity and support exacerbates their vulnerability, leading to long-lasting trauma and mental health issues. It is crucial for society to recognize and address these impacts, providing these girls with the necessary support systems to heal and rebuild their lives.

Fortunately, there are advocacy and support organizations in Mexico working tirelessly to help girls affected by early marriages. These organizations offer counseling, legal assistance, and educational programs to empower and uplift these girls. By amplifying the voices of survivors and sharing their narratives of resilience, we hope to inspire change and shine a light on the urgent need for societal reform.

"Unbreakable Spirits" showcases the narratives and stories of women who have escaped early marriages in Mexico. Their journeys of resilience, courage, and determination serve as a testament to the strength of the human spirit. Through their stories, we gain insights into the challenges they faced, the obstacles they overcame, and the hope they found in reclaiming their lives.

This subchapter aims to inform and educate everyone about the devastating effects of early marriages on young girls in Mexico. By shedding light on this issue, we hope to inspire empathy, ignite conversations, and mobilize action towards creating a society where every girl can flourish, free from the chains of early marriage.

Unbreakable Spirits

. . .

Emotional Trauma and Mental Health Challenges

In the subchapter "Emotional Trauma and Mental Health Challenges" of "Unbreakable Spirits: Narratives and Stories of Resilience from Women Who Have Escaped Early Marriages in Mexico," we delve into the profound emotional and psychological impacts experienced by young girls forced into early marriages in Mexico. This chapter aims to shed light on the devastating consequences of these forced unions, exploring the cultural significance of age disparities in Mexican marriages, the role of family and community in early weddings, and the need for advocacy and support organizations to aid girls affected by this practice.

The cultural significance of age disparities in Mexican marriages is deeply rooted in traditional gender roles and patriarchal norms. Historically, Mexican society has maintained a hierarchical structure where older men are seen as protectors and providers for younger women. However, this power dynamic often results in emotional and psychological trauma for the young girls involved. The chapter explores how these age disparities perpetuate a cycle of inequality and contribute to mental health challenges faced by these girls.

Furthermore, the role of family and community in early Mexican weddings is crucial to understanding the context in which these marriages occur. The chapter delves into the pressure placed on families to conform to societal expectations, leading them to marry off their young daughters. It also examines the lack of agency and support these girls receive, leaving them vulnerable to emotional trauma and mental health challenges.

To address the profound impacts of early marriages, advocacy and support organizations play a pivotal role. This subchapter highlights the efforts of various organizations working tirelessly to provide resources, counseling, and legal support to girls affected by this practice. By sharing their stories, we hope to inspire change and empower these young women to reclaim their lives and overcome the emotional and mental health challenges they face.

Finally, the subchapter presents narratives and stories of resilience from women who have escaped early marriages in Mexico. Their personal accounts serve as powerful testimonials of their strength, determination, and ability to heal. These stories not only provide hope and inspiration but also raise awareness about the urgent need for societal change to protect the rights and well-being of young girls in Mexico.

In conclusion, "Emotional Trauma and Mental Health Challenges" explores the devastating consequences of early marriages in Mexico. By examining the cultural significance of age disparities, the role of family and community, the need for advocacy and support organizations, and sharing narratives of resilience, this subchapter aims to educate and engage readers from all backgrounds, highlighting the urgent need for change and support for girls affected by early marriages in Mexico.

Struggles with Identity and Self-Worth

In the subchapter titled "Struggles with Identity and Self-Worth," we delve into the profound emotional and psychological impacts faced by young girls forced into early marriages in Mexico. This chapter sheds light on the multifaceted challenges these girls encounter as they navigate the complex terrain of identity and self-worth.

For many of these girls, the cultural significance of age disparities in Mexican marriages plays a significant role in shaping their sense of self. They are thrust into adult roles at a tender age, often before they have had the chance to form their own identities. As a result, they grapple with questions of who they are, what they want, and what their future holds.

Moreover, the role of family and community in early Mexican weddings further compounds these struggles. Familial expectations and societal pressures exert a heavy influence on these young girls, leaving them feeling trapped and devoid of agency. They are torn between the desire to conform to cultural norms and the longing for personal fulfillment and self-actualization.

Consequently, the emotional and psychological toll on these girls is immense. They experience a loss of childhood, forced to assume adult responsibilities without the necessary emotional maturity. Feelings of isolation, depression, and anxiety become their constant companions as they grapple with the weight of their circumstances.

However, amidst these struggles, there is hope. Advocacy and support organizations have emerged to help girls affected by early marriages in Mexico. These organizations provide a lifeline, offering emotional support, legal aid, and educational opportunities to empower these young women to reclaim their lives.

In "Unbreakable Spirits: Narratives and Stories of Resilience from Women Who Have Escaped Early Marriages in Mexico," we hear firsthand accounts of resilience and triumph. Through the stories of these courageous women, we gain insight into their journeys of self-discovery, healing, and reclaiming their identity and self-worth. Their narratives inspire us to challenge societal norms, advocate for change, and support those affected by early marriages.

This subchapter aims to raise awareness among everyone about the struggles faced by young girls forced into early marriages in Mexico. By shedding light on the emotional and psychological impacts, cultural context, and the role of support organizations, we hope to foster empathy, understanding, and action to bring about change. Together, we can create a society that values the rights and well-being of all its members, regardless of their age or gender.

Coping Mechanisms and Resilience in the Face of Adversity

Adversity can strike anyone at any time, and for young girls forced into early marriages in Mexico, the challenges can seem insurmountable. However, the human spirit is remarkably resilient, and time and time again, these women have shown incredible strength and determination in the face of adversity. This subchapter explores the coping mechanisms and resilience exhibited by women who have escaped early marriages in Mexico.

One of the most powerful coping mechanisms for these women is the support they receive from family and community. Despite being part of a culture that often perpetuates early marriages, many families and community members rally behind these girls, providing a support system that is crucial for their resilience. By having people who believe in them and stand by their side, these women gain the strength to break free from their oppressive situations.

Emotionally and psychologically, the impact of early marriages on young girls is profound. Many suffer from low self-esteem, depression, and a sense of hopelessness. However, through various coping mechanisms, they have managed to overcome these challenges. Some have found solace in creative outlets such as art, writing, or music, using these mediums to express their emotions and find a sense of identity in their new-found freedom. Others have turned to education, using knowledge as a weapon against the oppressive forces that once controlled their lives.

Advocacy and support organizations play a crucial role in helping these women rebuild their lives. These organizations

Unbreakable Spirits

provide a safe space for them to share their stories, connect with others who have gone through similar experiences, and access resources such as legal aid, counseling, and educational opportunities. By providing a platform for these women to voice their struggles and triumphs, these organizations empower them to become advocates for change and break the cycle of early marriages in Mexico.

The narratives and stories of resilience from women who have escaped early marriages in Mexico are both inspiring and heart-wrenching. These stories serve as a reminder of the incredible strength of the human spirit and the power of resilience. By sharing their experiences, these women not only find healing and closure but also provide hope and inspiration to others who may be trapped in similar situations.

In conclusion, coping mechanisms and resilience are crucial for women who have escaped early marriages in Mexico. Through the support of family and community, the exploration of creative outlets, the pursuit of education, and the assistance of advocacy and support organizations, these women have managed to overcome the emotional and psychological impacts of early marriages. Their narratives and stories serve as a testament to the power of the human spirit and the possibility of a brighter future for all those affected by early marriages in Mexico.

Chapter Four
Advocacy and Support Organizations for Girls Affected by Early Marriages in Mexico

Legal Framework and Initiatives to Combat Early Marriages

The prevalence of early marriages in Mexico is a grave concern that requires urgent attention. This subchapter explores the legal framework and initiatives that aim to combat this harmful practice. By understanding the cultural significance of age disparities in Mexican marriages, the role of family and community in early weddings, as well as the emotional and psychological impacts on young girls, we can work towards creating a safer and healthier future for these girls. Additionally, we will highlight advocacy and support organizations that aid girls affected by early marriages and share inspiring narratives and stories of resilience from women who have escaped such marriages.

Legal Framework

Mexico has taken significant steps to address early marriages through legislation. The minimum age of marriage has been raised to 18 for both girls and boys, in compliance with international standards set by the Convention on the Rights of the Child. However, despite these legal provisions, child marriages still persist due to cultural factors and lack of enforcement.

Initiatives to Combat Early Marriages

To combat early marriages, various initiatives have been implemented in Mexico. These include comprehensive sexuality education programs in schools, community awareness campaigns, and the establishment of support centers for at-risk girls. These initiatives aim to educate communities about the consequences of early marriages and empower girls to make informed decisions about their lives.

The Cultural Significance of Age Disparities

In Mexican society, age disparities in marriages have cultural significance and are often rooted in gender inequality. It is essential to understand these cultural norms and challenge them by promoting gender equality and women's empowerment. By addressing the underlying social norms that perpetuate early marriages, we can work towards creating a society where girls are able to choose their own futures.

The Role of Family and Community

Family and community play a significant role in early Mexican weddings. Traditional norms and pressures from relatives can force young girls into marriages against their will. However, efforts are being made to engage families and communities in discussions about the harmful effects of early marriages, encouraging them to support girls' education and delay marriage until they are ready.

Unbreakable Spirits

. . .

Emotional and Psychological Impacts

Forced into adulthood prematurely, young girls forced into early marriages face emotional and psychological challenges. These include limited opportunities for education, increased vulnerability to domestic violence, and mental health issues. Addressing these impacts requires a comprehensive approach that provides counseling, education, and economic empowerment to girls affected by early marriages.

Advocacy and Support Organizations

Several advocacy and support organizations in Mexico are dedicated to combating early marriages and providing assistance to affected girls. These organizations offer safe spaces, legal advice, counseling, and educational opportunities to empower girls and help them escape from early marriages.

Narratives and Stories of Resilience

The stories of women who have escaped early marriages in Mexico serve as powerful examples of resilience and determination. These narratives highlight the importance of education, community support, and self-belief in breaking free from the cycle of early marriages. By sharing these stories, we aim to inspire others and create a collective movement against this harmful practice.

The fight against early marriages in Mexico requires a multifaceted approach that addresses legal, cultural, and societal factors. By understanding the legal framework, initiatives, and the cultural significance of age disparities, we can work towards creating a society where girls are not forced into early marriages. Through advocacy, support organizations, and sharing narratives of resilience, we can empower girls and provide them with the tools to build a brighter future. Ultimately, it is the responsibility of everyone to create a world where every girl can grow, learn, and thrive, free from the shackles of early marriages.

Non-Governmental Organizations and Their Efforts

In the fight against early marriages in Mexico, non-governmental organizations (NGOs) have played a crucial role in advocating for the rights and well-being of young girls. These organizations are committed to raising awareness, providing support, and empowering girls who have been forced into early marriages.

The cultural significance of age disparities in Mexican marriages is deeply rooted in tradition and societal norms. However, NGOs are working tirelessly to challenge these norms and bring about a shift in attitudes. By engaging with communities and promoting dialogue, they aim to educate people about the detrimental effects of early marriages on girls' physical, emotional, and psychological well-being.

Family and community play a significant role in early Mexican weddings. While it can be challenging to change deeply ingrained practices, NGOs strive to create a supportive environment within families and communities. They provide counseling and education to parents, encouraging them to prioritize their daughters' education and personal development over early marriages. By engaging community leaders and influencers, these organizations are able to spread their message effectively and bring about change at a grassroots level.

The emotional and psychological impacts on young girls forced into early marriages are profound. Many of these girls face a loss of agency, limited access to education, and a higher risk of domestic violence. NGOs provide vital emotional support and counseling to help these girls heal and rebuild their lives.

Unbreakable Spirits

They create safe spaces where survivors can share their experiences and find solace in the company of others who have gone through similar ordeals.

Advocacy and support organizations for girls affected by early marriages in Mexico are working tirelessly to provide a comprehensive range of services. They offer legal aid to survivors, ensuring that perpetrators are held accountable and justice is served. These organizations also provide vocational training and financial assistance to help survivors become self-sufficient and break free from the cycle of poverty.

"Unbreakable Spirits: Narratives and Stories of Resilience from Women Who Have Escaped Early Marriages in Mexico" showcases the strength and resilience of women who have escaped early marriages. Through these narratives, readers gain insight into the challenges these women have faced and the triumphs they have achieved. By sharing their stories, the book aims to inspire others and create a sense of solidarity among survivors.

In conclusion, NGOs are playing a vital role in addressing the issue of early marriages in Mexico. Through their efforts, they are challenging cultural norms, providing support to survivors, and advocating for the rights of young girls. With their unwavering dedication, these organizations are paving the way for a brighter and more equitable future for girls in Mexico.

Access to Education and Empowerment Programs

Education is a fundamental human right and a powerful tool for empowerment. Unfortunately, many young girls in Mexico face significant barriers to accessing education due to early marriages. In this subchapter, we will explore the importance of providing access to education and empowerment programs for these girls, and how they can help break the cycle of early marriages and promote resilience.

Christine Groethe

The cultural significance of age disparities in Mexican marriages is deeply rooted in tradition and societal norms. However, it is essential to critically examine these practices and understand the negative consequences they have on young girls. By marrying at a young age, these girls are deprived of educational opportunities, limiting their potential and perpetuating the cycle of poverty. By highlighting the cultural significance of age disparities, we can begin to challenge these harmful practices and advocate for change.

Family and community play a significant role in early Mexican weddings, often pressuring young girls into marriage. It is crucial to engage with families and communities to raise awareness about the importance of education and the potential harm caused by early marriages. By involving them in discussions and empowering them with knowledge, we can encourage a shift in attitudes and behaviors, ultimately leading to the protection of girls' rights and increased access to education.

The emotional and psychological impacts on young girls forced into early marriages in Mexico are devastating. They often face isolation, abuse, and a loss of autonomy. Empowerment programs that combine education, counseling, and skill-building can help these girls regain their sense of self-worth and build a brighter future. By addressing the emotional and psychological needs of these girls, we can support their resilience and assist them in overcoming the trauma they have experienced.

Advocacy and support organizations play a crucial role in protecting the rights of girls affected by early marriages in Mexico. These organizations provide a safe space for girls to share their stories, seek support, and access resources. By highlighting the work of these organizations, we can encourage community involvement, fundraising efforts, and policy changes to better protect the rights of these girls.

Finally, this subchapter will share narratives and stories of resilience from women who have escaped early marriages in

Unbreakable Spirits

Mexico. These stories serve as powerful testimonials of strength and courage, inspiring others to believe in their own ability to break free from the cycle of early marriages. By sharing these narratives, we hope to shed light on the challenges faced by these women and celebrate their triumphs as they reclaim their lives through education and empowerment.

In conclusion, providing access to education and empowerment programs is vital in combating early marriages in Mexico. By addressing the cultural significance of age disparities, engaging with families and communities, supporting the emotional and psychological well-being of girls, and promoting advocacy and support organizations, we can empower these girls to transcend the limitations imposed on them. Through narratives and stories of resilience, we can inspire others to join the fight against early marriages and create a better future for all.

Challenges and Future Directions for Advocacy

The cultural significance of age disparities in Mexican marriages, the role of family and community in early Mexican weddings, emotional and psychological impacts on young girls forced into early marriages in Mexico, advocacy and support organizations for girls affected by early marriages in Mexico, and narratives and stories of resilience from women who have escaped early marriages in Mexico are all crucial aspects that demand attention and action. This subchapter explores the challenges faced in advocacy efforts and outlines future directions to address the issue effectively.

Advocating against early marriages in Mexico encounters several challenges. One of the primary hurdles is the deeply ingrained cultural significance of age disparities in Mexican marriages. Traditional norms perpetuate the belief that girls should marry at a young age, often to significantly older men. Overcoming this deep-rooted cultural belief requires a multifaceted approach that involves engaging with communities, religious leaders, and families to challenge and transform these norms.

Additionally, the role of family and community in early Mexican weddings poses another challenge. In many cases, families play an active role in arranging these marriages, often prioritizing economic considerations or societal expectations over the well-being and agency of young girls. Advocacy efforts must involve engaging with families, educating them about the harmful consequences of early marriages, and providing alternative perspectives that empower girls to make informed choices.

The emotional and psychological impacts on young girls forced into early marriages in Mexico cannot be underestimated. These girls often face immense trauma, including physical and sexual abuse, limited education opportunities, and restricted personal development. Advocacy efforts must prioritize addressing the mental health needs of these girls, providing access to trauma-informed counseling, and creating safe spaces where they can share their experiences and find support.

To effectively advocate for change, it is crucial to identify and collaborate with existing advocacy and support organizations for girls affected by early marriages in Mexico. These organizations play a pivotal role in providing direct assistance, raising awareness, and advocating for policy reforms. Future directions for advocacy involve strengthening these collaborations, supporting their initiatives, and fostering a collective effort to amplify the voices of those affected.

Finally, the subchapter explores narratives and stories of resilience from women who have escaped early marriages in Mexico. These stories serve as powerful tools for advocacy, shedding light on the injustices faced by young girls and inspiring action. By sharing these narratives widely, the subchapter aims to create empathy, raise awareness, and mobilize a collective response to end early marriages in Mexico.

Unbreakable Spirits

In conclusion, addressing the challenges related to early marriages in Mexico requires comprehensive advocacy efforts. By challenging cultural norms, engaging with families and communities, addressing the emotional and psychological impacts, collaborating with support organizations, and sharing narratives of resilience, we can work towards a future where every girl in Mexico has the opportunity to thrive and fulfill her potential. Together, we can break the cycle of early marriages and create a society that values and protects the rights of young girls.

Chapter Five
Narratives and Stories of Resilience from Women Who Have Escaped Early Marriages in Mexico

Sharing Personal Experiences and Overcoming Stigma
In this subchapter, we delve into the powerful narratives and stories of resilience from women who have escaped early marriages in Mexico. These personal experiences shed light on the cultural significance of age disparities in Mexican marriages, the role of family and community in early Mexican weddings, the emotional and psychological impacts on young girls forced into early marriages, as well as the advocacy and support organizations available for girls affected by this issue.

The cultural significance of age disparities in Mexican marriages is deeply rooted in tradition and societal norms. Many girls are married off at a young age to older men, often due to economic reasons or as a means to preserve family honor. By sharing their personal experiences, these women provide an intimate look into the complexities of these age disparities and the impact they have on both the girls and the wider community.

Family and community play a crucial role in early Mexican weddings. Often, it is the pressure from family members and the community that forces young girls into marriages against their will. These personal accounts shed light on the dynamics within families and communities, the expectations placed on young girls, and the challenges they face when trying to break free from these traditions.

The emotional and psychological impacts on young girls forced into early marriages are profound and long-lasting. These women share their stories of fear, isolation, and loss of agency, as well as the struggles they faced in rebuilding their lives after escaping these marriages. Through their narratives, we gain a deeper understanding of the mental health consequences and the resilience required to overcome the trauma associated with early marriages.

Fortunately, there are advocacy and support organizations dedicated to helping girls affected by early marriages in Mexico. These organizations provide safe spaces, counseling, education, and legal support to empower these girls and help them rebuild their lives. By highlighting these organizations, we aim to raise awareness and encourage support for their crucial work.

Ultimately, the narratives and stories of resilience shared by these women serve as a source of inspiration and empowerment for others facing similar challenges. Their journeys of overcoming stigma and rebuilding their lives serve as a reminder of the strength of the human spirit and the importance of fighting for change. Through their stories, we hope to ignite conversations, challenge societal norms, and create a more inclusive and supportive environment for all women in Mexico.

Journey to Freedom and Reclaiming Independence

In the subchapter, "Journey to Freedom and Reclaiming Independence," we delve into the inspiring stories of women who have escaped early marriages in Mexico. These narratives of resilience shed light on the cultural significance of age disparities in Mexican marriages, the role of family and community in early weddings, the emotional and psychological impacts on

Unbreakable Spirits

young girls forced into such marriages, and the advocacy and support organizations available to help these girls reclaim their independence.

Mexico, a country rich in tradition and cultural heritage, has long grappled with the issue of early marriages. These marriages often involve significant age disparities, with young girls being married off to much older men. In this subchapter, we explore the reasons behind this cultural practice and its implications for the girls involved. We examine the societal norms and expectations that perpetuate these marriages, challenging the audience to consider the cultural significance of age disparities in Mexican unions.

Furthermore, we delve into the crucial role that family and community play in early weddings. We explore the pressures and expectations placed on families, as well as the limited options available to young girls who may wish to resist such marriages. By examining the dynamics within families and communities, we aim to provide a deeper understanding of the complex factors that contribute to the continuation of early marriages in Mexico.

The emotional and psychological impacts on young girls forced into early marriages cannot be ignored. We highlight the struggles faced by these girls, including the loss of educational opportunities, limited agency, and the psychological toll of being married before they are ready. By sharing their stories, we hope to raise awareness about the long-lasting effects of early marriages on the mental well-being of these girls.

This subchapter also sheds light on the advocacy and support organizations that exist to help girls affected by early marriages in Mexico. We provide information on various organizations that work tirelessly to empower these girls, offer them support and guidance, and help them navigate the challenges they face in reclaiming their independence.

Finally, "Journey to Freedom and Reclaiming Independence" features narratives and stories of resilience from women who have escaped early marriages in Mexico. These powerful accounts showcase the strength, determination, and resilience of these women as they fought against societal norms and reclaimed their independence. By sharing their stories, we hope to inspire others and foster a sense of empathy and understanding.

This subchapter serves as a call to action for everyone, urging them to reflect on the cultural significance of age disparities in Mexican marriages, the role of family and community, the emotional and psychological impacts on young girls, the importance of advocacy and support organizations, and the narratives of resilience from women who have escaped early marriages in Mexico. It is our hope that through understanding and awareness, we can work together to bring about positive change and empower young girls to live lives free from the constraints of early marriages.

Empowering Others and Breaking the Cycle

In a society where age disparities in marriages are deeply ingrained, it is crucial to examine the cultural significance of such unions in Mexico. This subchapter delves into the complexities surrounding early marriages and highlights the need for empowerment and breaking the cycle.

The role of family and community cannot be understated when discussing early Mexican weddings. Often, these unions are arranged by parents and elders who believe they are safeguarding their daughters' futures. However, it is essential to question the long-term implications of such decisions. By exploring the perspectives of both families and communities, we can better understand the societal structures that perpetuate early marriages.

Beyond the physical aspects, the emotional and psychological impacts on young girls forced into early marriages in

Unbreakable Spirits

Mexico are profound. These girls are robbed of their childhood and the opportunity to pursue education and personal growth. Their dreams and aspirations are often discarded, leaving them vulnerable to long-lasting trauma and mental health issues. By shedding light on these impacts, we hope to raise awareness and inspire action to protect the well-being of these young girls.

Addressing the issue of early marriages requires the collaboration of advocacy and support organizations. In this subchapter, we highlight the crucial work being done by these organizations in Mexico. They provide a lifeline for girls affected by early marriages, offering support, education, and resources to help them break free from the cycle of abuse and inequality. By showcasing their efforts, we hope to encourage readers to support and engage with these organizations to create lasting change.

The heart of this subchapter lies in the narratives and stories of resilience from women who have escaped early marriages in Mexico. These stories are a testament to the strength and courage of these women, who defied societal norms and overcame immense obstacles. Through their experiences, we gain insight into the struggles they faced, the resilience they cultivated, and the transformative power of empowerment.

Ultimately, the subchapter "Empowering Others and Breaking the Cycle" serves as a call to action for everyone. It invites readers to reflect on the cultural significance of age disparities in Mexican marriages, the role of family and community, the emotional and psychological impacts on young girls, and the importance of advocacy and support organizations. By amplifying the voices of those who have escaped early marriages, we hope to inspire change, foster empathy, and ultimately create a society where every girl can grow, thrive, and fulfill her dreams.

. . .

Christine Groethe

Lessons Learned and Inspiring Change for Future Generations

In the subchapter titled "Lessons Learned and Inspiring Change for Future Generations," we delve into the profound impact of early marriages on young girls in Mexico. This chapter aims to enlighten everyone about the cultural significance of age disparities in Mexican marriages, the role of family and community in early weddings, the emotional and psychological impacts on young girls, advocacy and support organizations available, and most importantly, narratives and stories of resilience from women who have escaped early marriages in Mexico.

The cultural significance of age disparities in Mexican marriages cannot be understated. For centuries, Mexican society has upheld traditional values and norms that perpetuate the idea of girls being married off at a young age. We explore the historical roots of this practice and shed light on the consequences it has on the lives of these young girls.

Furthermore, we delve into the role of family and community in early Mexican weddings. We examine the pressures and expectations placed on families, their motivations, and the societal structures that enable such marriages. Understanding these dynamics is crucial in order to bring about meaningful change.

The emotional and psychological impacts on young girls forced into early marriages in Mexico are heart-wrenching. We explore the trauma and challenges they face, ranging from limited educational opportunities and economic dependence to domestic violence and stifled personal growth. By shedding light on these issues, we hope to foster empathy and understanding in our readers.

Advocacy and support organizations play a crucial role in addressing the needs of girls affected by early marriages in Mexico. We highlight the work of these organizations, the services they provide, and the impact they have on empowering young girls to escape these harmful unions.

Unbreakable Spirits

Finally, the narratives and stories of resilience from women who have escaped early marriages in Mexico serve as a beacon of hope. We share inspiring firsthand accounts of these women who defied societal expectations and fought for their freedom. Their stories are a testament to the indomitable spirit and strength of the human will.

By addressing these topics, we aim to raise awareness, challenge cultural norms, and inspire change for future generations. This subchapter serves as a call to action for everyone, encouraging them to stand against early marriages and support the empowerment of young girls in Mexico. Together, we can create a future where no girl's dreams are shattered, and every woman's spirit remains unbreakable.

Conclusion
A Call to Action for Ending Early Marriages in Mexico

Summary of Key Findings and Insights

In the book "Unbreakable Spirits: Narratives and Stories of Resilience from Women Who Have Escaped Early Marriages in Mexico," we delve into the deeply rooted cultural significance of age disparities in Mexican marriages, the role of family and community in early Mexican weddings, the emotional and psychological impacts on young girls forced into early marriages, advocacy and support organizations for girls affected by early marriages, and most importantly, the narratives and stories of resilience from women who have escaped such marriages.

One of the key findings of this book is the cultural significance of age disparities in Mexican marriages. It explores how the patriarchal tradition of older men marrying young girls is deeply embedded in Mexican society, perpetuating power imbalances and limiting the opportunities for young girls. By examining this phenomenon, we aim to shed light on the need for social change and the empowerment of young girls.

Furthermore, the book examines the role of family and community in early Mexican weddings. It highlights how soci-

Christine Groethe

etal norms, family pressure, and community expectations often contribute to the perpetuation of early marriages. By understanding the intricate dynamics at play, we hope to encourage dialogue and awareness among families and communities, fostering an environment that promotes the well-being and agency of young girls.

Another important aspect explored in this book is the emotional and psychological impacts on young girls forced into early marriages. Through personal accounts and psychological research, we uncover the traumatic experiences these girls endure, including the loss of education, limited opportunities, and the denial of their own agency. By raising awareness about these impacts, we aim to advocate for better support systems and resources for these girls.

Advocacy and support organizations for girls affected by early marriages in Mexico are also highlighted in this book. We provide valuable information about the various organizations working tirelessly to provide support, education, and empowerment to these young girls. By showcasing their efforts, we hope to inspire others to get involved and contribute to the cause.

Finally, the heart of this book lies in the narratives and stories of resilience from women who have escaped early marriages in Mexico. By sharing their personal stories, these brave women provide hope and inspiration to others who may be trapped in similar situations. Through their resilience, they demonstrate the strength of the human spirit and the potential for change.

In conclusion, "Unbreakable Spirits" offers a comprehensive exploration of the cultural significance of age disparities in Mexican marriages, the role of family and community, the emotional and psychological impacts on young girls, advocacy and support organizations, and the narratives of resilient women. This book is a call to action for everyone to understand, support, and empower young girls affected by early marriages in Mexico.

. . .

Unbreakable Spirits

Importance of Collaboration between Government, Communities, and Individuals

In the fight against early marriages in Mexico, collaboration between the government, communities, and individuals is of utmost importance. This subchapter delves into the significance of this collaboration and how it can make a difference in the lives of young girls affected by early marriages.

The cultural significance of age disparities in Mexican marriages cannot be overlooked. It is deeply rooted in tradition and often seen as a way to preserve family honor and stability. However, through collaboration, we can challenge these cultural norms and educate communities about the negative consequences of early marriages. By working together, we can promote a shift in cultural attitudes and beliefs, and encourage acceptance of alternative paths for young girls.

The role of family and community in early Mexican weddings is crucial. Often, it is the pressure from these close-knit groups that forces young girls into marriages against their will. By fostering collaboration between the government, communities, and individuals, we can create a support system that empowers families and communities to make informed decisions, and to prioritize the well-being and future prospects of young girls.

The emotional and psychological impacts on young girls forced into early marriages in Mexico are devastating. Many suffer from depression, anxiety, and low self-esteem, as they are robbed of their childhood and the opportunity to pursue education and personal growth. Collaboration is essential in providing these girls with the necessary emotional support and counseling services. By working together, we can create safe spaces where they can heal and rebuild their lives.

Advocacy and support organizations for girls affected by early marriages in Mexico play a vital role in raising awareness.

Testimonial I
Maria´s story

Betrothal

In a small, sun-soaked village nestled amidst the rolling hills of Mexico, young Maria found herself at the center of a decision that would shape the course of her life. At the tender age of 13, she stood on the precipice of a future chosen not by her own desires, but by the traditions of her culture and the expectations of her family.

It was a warm afternoon when her parents called her into the dimly lit living room of their modest adobe home. Maria's heart pounded in her chest as she walked toward them, her gaze fixed on the colorful tapestries that adorned the walls. Her parents exchanged knowing glances, their faces etched with a mixture of determination and sadness.

"Maria," her father began, his voice heavy with the weight of the decision he was about to reveal, "we have something important to discuss."

Maria nodded, her dark eyes wide with curiosity and a hint of apprehension. She had heard whispers in the village about the possibility of her betrothal, but she never imagined it would come so soon.

"You know our traditions, Maria," her mother added gently, her voice trembling. "It is time for you to be betrothed to Juan, the son of our neighbors. The arrangement has been made, and it is for the good of our family."

Maria's heart sank as the reality of her situation began to sink in. She had played with Juan in the fields as children, but she had never imagined that their youthful games would lead to such a binding commitment. Tears welled up in her eyes as she realized that her fate had been sealed without her consent.

The Weight of Expectations

As the days passed, Maria struggled to come to terms with her impending marriage. She was a child, not yet a woman, and the thought of becoming a wife and mother at such a young age weighed heavily on her shoulders. The village buzzed with anticipation, and well-meaning neighbors and relatives offered their congratulations, but Maria couldn't shake the feeling of helplessness that had settled deep within her.

With each passing day, her responsibilities grew. She was taught the art of homemaking, from cooking and cleaning to caring for the family's modest herd of goats. Her mother, a kind but stern woman, instructed her in the ways of a wife, emphasizing the importance of obedience and submission to her future husband.

Maria's childhood dreams of exploring the world beyond the village seemed increasingly distant, replaced by the reality of her role as a future wife and mother. She couldn't help but wonder about the adventures she might have had, the dreams she might have pursued, if she had been given a choice in the matter.

The Arrival of Womanhood

Months turned into years, and Maria's 13-year-old frame slowly began to mature. The arrival of womanhood brought with it a sense of inevitability and a growing sense of dread. She knew that the day of her marriage was drawing near, and she felt unprepared for the responsibilities that awaited her.

As her body changed, so did her understanding of the world around her. She watched other girls in the village, some of whom were already married and with children of their own, and couldn't help but feel a sense of envy for the freedom they had lost. The dreams she had once held so dear seemed to slip further and further away.

Despite her reservations, Maria tried to find solace in the knowledge that her parents believed they were doing what was best for her. She knew that the arranged marriage was born out of love and concern for her future, but it was a future that felt out of her control.

As the day of her wedding approached, Maria couldn't help but wonder what lay ahead for her as a young bride, and how the early arranged marriage, before the bloom of puberty, would continue to shape her life in a world where tradition and family expectations held such sway.

Testimonial II
Jessica's Story

The Decision

Jessica sat on the porch of her family's cozy farmhouse, the warm Chihuahua sun kissing her cheeks. She gazed out at the vast, rolling fields that stretched as far as the eye could see, and the mountains that loomed in the distance. It was a view she had grown up with, one that had always felt like home.

But today, as she watched her family working together in the fields, tending to the crops and caring for the livestock, she couldn't help but feel a sense of restlessness deep within her. At fifteen, Jessica was at a crossroads in her life. Her parents had arranged a marriage for her to a young man from a neighboring farm, and she couldn't stop thinking about what her future would hold.

She loved her family dearly, and the thought of leaving them behind was heart-wrenching. Her parents had explained that this was a tradition in their community, that she would be starting her own family soon, and that it was a path that had been followed by generations before her. But Jessica couldn't shake the feeling that there was more to life than what she had always known.

As the sun began to set, casting a warm, golden glow over the landscape, Jessica made a decision. She would talk to her parents about her doubts and fears, about her desire for something different in her life. She knew it wouldn't be easy, but she couldn't ignore the yearning in her heart any longer.

A Heartfelt Conversation

That evening, after a hearty dinner with her family, Jessica found herself sitting with her parents in their dimly lit living room. The air was thick with tension as she tried to find the right words to express her feelings.

"Mom, Dad," she began, her voice quivering with nervousness, "I need to talk to you about something important."

Her parents exchanged worried glances, but her father nodded for her to continue. "Go ahead, mija," he said gently.

Jessica took a deep breath. "I've been thinking a lot about the future, about the life you've planned for me with Carlos. I know it's a tradition in our community, and I love you both so much for wanting what's best for me, but I can't help feeling like there's more to life than what we have here."

Her mother reached out and took Jessica's hand, her eyes filled with understanding. "We want you to be happy, Jessica," she said softly.

Tears welled up in Jessica's eyes as she continued, "I want to explore the world, see new places, and maybe even go to school. I want to find out who I am beyond being a wife and mother. I hope you can understand."

Her father sighed and looked down at the floor for a moment before meeting her gaze. "Jessica, we want what's best for you, too," he said. "But you know that the life we have here is not an easy one. It's a life of hard work and sacrifice, but it's also a life filled with love and community. We worry about what might happen to you out there on your own."

Jessica nodded, her heart heavy with the weight of her decision. "I know it won't be easy, but I need to follow my own path, even if it takes me away from here for a while."

Setting Out

In the days that followed their conversation, Jessica's parents came to accept her decision, though it was not without tears and worries. They understood that their daughter needed to find her own way in the world, and they wished her nothing but happiness.

With their blessing, Jessica packed a small bag with her most cherished belongings and said her tearful goodbyes to her family. She knew that leaving them behind was one of the hardest things she would ever do, but she also knew it was necessary for her own growth and self-discovery.

As she stood at the edge of their farm, looking out at the horizon, Jessica felt a mix of emotions – fear, excitement, and determination. She knew that the path she had chosen wouldn't be easy, but she was ready to face whatever challenges lay ahead.

With a deep breath, she took her first step toward a future that was uncertain but full of possibilities. Jessica was no longer just a daughter of the land; she was now a young woman on a journey to find her own place in the world.

Made in the USA
Las Vegas, NV
02 April 2025